SWALLOW

SWALLOW

Copyright © 2021 by Sam Rush

Cover art: "BaroqueIkebana" by Nicklas Hultman, used with permission.

Cover design by Matthew Radwan.

Author photo by Matthew Radwan.

Sibling Rivalry Press, LLC
PO Box 26147
Little Rock, AR 72221

info@siblingrivalrypress.com

www.siblingrivalrypress.com

ISBN: 978-1-943977-82-6

Library of Congress Control Number: 2020948988

By special invitation, this title is housed in the Rare Book and Special Collections Vault of the Library of Congress.

First Sibling Rivalry Press Edition, February 2021

SWALLOW

Sam Rush

Laura,
I can't wait
to read your
book!
M Sam

SIBLING RIVALRY PRESS
DISTURB/ENRAPTURE
LITTLE ROCK, ARKANSAS

Meaning

introduce into the body

a quantity consumed at one time
mouthful
throatful

any bird member of the family *Hirundinidae*
exhibiting the characteristic forked tail & long pointed wings

believe

accept
accept / as fact
accept / without resistance

alternative to spit

take in
envelope
example.
the night (   )s the valley

                      the boy
                      the valley beneath the boy
           the valley (   )ed the ocean
once

           the ocean will (   ) the rest but for the bird

drown

inundate

use up

absorb

utter (words) indistinctly
example.
what
EXAMPLE.
what
nevermind

retract
take back

assimilate

absorb
absorb / without protest
absorb /without / anymore / protest

introduce into the body / often / by way of mouth

keep from showing / as in / emotion
repress
consume (food/drink)

(cause/allow) to pass down one's throat

cause to pass down one's throat

allow to pass down one's throat

introduce into the body / often
indistinctly / nevermind
keep from showing / as in

a bird fork-tailed wings pointed
known portend to sailors of safe journey home
for how it will return each year to nest
or will not stray too far from shore
or how it feeds itself with insects caught on the wing
one life safe above the (   )ing sea into the other
for how no journey home or otherwise
would last the week without someone to (   )

contents

Sonnet for eating
& hormone injection

My mother coughed & I fell off & walked.
I take a bird & turn it into me.
I grow too broad & run to give it back.
Once. I ran so far I set a honeyed
turkey free. I my built sinew of you.
I swallowed the world & made myself more.
I didn't brand my body beaker just
to prove some glass more noble than the mirror.
Once. I spit my downy into bottles,
sped & spilt me out the open windows.
I used to leave me strewn, highwayside.
So who's to say there hasn't been some vial
of me waiting out beyond my brink of skin.
Who's to say I wouldn't take me in.

Sonnet for cock sucking & baptism

Forgive me, Lord. For I have a mouth full
of dicks & not all of them organic.
Forgive me the virgin coconut oil
in lieu of water-based lube like I think
I'm better than that or some shit.
Anointed, dick. I grease the word & slick
my tongue in it. Let all I lap be wrapped
& swaddled in. I spit & poof: Magic.
Watch the plastic twitch. Lord, inside my salve
your accidents grow stiff. Suck fist to dick.
The knuckle, dick. I laughed, Dick Midas, now
the sky is dick. I sing my lips to dick.
I speak the name you chose yourself
aloud & don't we feel it, every inch.

The Spandrels of San Marco

Two rounded archways, built adjacent, will form above them an empty,
v-shaped space. That space is called a spandrel. *Evolutionary biologists borrow*
the term to describe a trait that has no functional value, but is the byproduct of
selection for a useful adaptation. Your tailless tailbone: spandrel. *Nipples that*
don't lactate: spandrel.

Anthropologists suggest that our human tendency towards belief in the
supernatural results from selection for a trait called agent detection—*our*
ability to assign motive to that which exists outside ourselves,
to imagine a story that fills the empty space around a Why— *that belief in God*
is nothing more than an evolutionary accident, left over space around a useful
adaptation, a spandrel.

Spandrel:

Once a man held me in his arms
like a question mark

for the first time I wished two objects
could exist with no space between them

Spandrel:

My father taught me grief is like a hole
inside of you

Mourning does not fill the hole
it is simply how we learn to live around it

Spandrel:

When I was fifteen God or something like it
plucked a hole in me

My hearing began to drip out slowly
leaving behind an empty space

The space filled with a piercing ring
that aches & wakes me in the night

I learned to love from story boys with waking
boomboxes held above their heads & pillars of salt

The story goes love is love when it turns its object's
name into a seraphim, their voice into a prayer

Spandrel:

Sometimes I hear voices in the ringing

Sometimes I hear the voice of the man
who held me a question mark

Sometimes I hear the voice of God
Sometimes I cannot tell the difference

Spandrel:

The thing about love & death is that both turn
humans into gods without asking

Spandrel:

Sometimes I hear voices in the ringing

Sometimes the creak of the rope he lost to
in a quarry outside Cincinnati

I do not know the shape of it
I imagine a gaping empty space

Spandrel:

I do not wish to make
this man a god

I do not wish to erase the callous in his voice
or the careless moments of greed

I do not wish to write him into my own mythology
to absolve an empty space

The incidental space of the spandrels
at San Marco's Bascillica in Venice, Italy

are filled and blooming
with delicate portraits of angels

Onlookers crane their necks
to gaze upon them & upward

towards heaven
& forget the ground

Spandrel:

Once I fell in love the way the story goes
& forgot my own name

The story goes you will be loved
into a whole

The story goes you are born
with a hole inside you

the shape of your lover's arm
or ear or crooked neck

The story goes you will look upon your lover
& see heaven in their eyes

Spandrel:

I do not wish to forget
your eyes for heaven

Spandrel:

I do not wish for a love that cranes my neck
upwards & away from this earth

Spandrel:

I try to hold myself at night like a question mark
but cannot coax my body into arching

because it is harder for me to imagine a story
that ends in a trans body coming

than it is for me to imagine a story
that ends in a trans body coming back from the dead

Spandrel:

I am afraid to be loved
like a symbol

Spandrel:

I am afraid to be loved
like a myth

Spandrel:

I am afraid of a love that will turn me false god
only to prove me fallacy

Spandrel:

There are voices in the ringing
 In the silence there is a song

& I know he is not waiting for me
out there in the gaping air

but I swear
I swear to god

I hear something

Sonnet for speech too soft & you who've yet to choose a name

Once. A bell tolled & tolled & I am told
does still. Once. I took a man at eyes &
out his mouth a stack of breath fainted, lay
still & still hot & silent at my feet.
Once. There was a last whisper that found me.
A word & a voice skipped like stone across
a surface split to sound circles in circles
of declaration, each fading flat in time
to meet my skin. I mean. My mother
speaks to angels. I mean. Today I keep
the speaker out of me for long enough
to watch a Swallow swoon the ghost of song.
I mean. That I have come to trust the sound
of you, Child, whatever we have yet to hear.

Sonnet for *phobia*
& why we waste away

Theory: God made a mouth at both ends
& me a hunger ripped between. Theory:
Fear wakes up inside the wrong body.
How does it leave. Theory: A boy. Swallows
a girl to keep them both from starving. Theory:
We dress our tongues in tongues & disappear
around their kneading. This is the same.
Replace the tongues with nothing. Theory:
We were raised sirens in a soundproof room.
I didn't lose my hearing. I let it choke
a prayer to continuity. Theory:
There is one scream. There has only ever
been one scream. My mouth is a pipeline out.
My mouth is a tributary. Bursting.

Sonnet for sonic feedback
& media representation

I want to watch us fucking on tv.
I mean. I've seen the snake, its ass inside
its gape & named the way we hunger
or whatever. For whatever a mouth
awake inside another mouth would say.
Would see. My hearing aids scream whenever
you come close to me. Sound a sound swallowing
its tail to tell out louder, still. Tell me
a story. Tell me a story, one where
the boy like us repeats himself. Wakes. Wakes.
& keeps doing it. Walks home & walks home,
again. Looks & looks up & on the screen
sees himself take in something like himself
& grow louder, still. Louder, still. Louder

TV is making shows about gay teenagers & I still can't masturbate to the cowboy movie because my body requires a more plausible argument as to why I'm in the room

A boy is an argument. A boy in a boy's mouth is an argument. This is a statement. This is a thesis statement. A thesis statement is followed by support. A boy is a sentence. *Can I be the verb* asks the boy. The boy asks the boy this. One of these things is not like the other. One of these others is not quite the thing. Other than that there's another thing that's not the boy & not the other boy & since you can see either can't you figure out the rest. This is a question. This lives in the mouth? This is a question. This lives in the body until the body throws it out. A thesis statement lives in the mouth for six months before hatching & getting a real jaw & still using your Netflix password. *Can I be the password* asks the boy. A password is a thesis statement. A thesis statement is followed by a story with a wink & a bottom lip & in the end the boy gets the boy. The word boy. The word *boy*. Which one is the thesis statement? A thesis statement is a story that lives inside a boy's mouth. I was a boy once. A statement. *I was a boy once.* A thesis statement. A thesis statement is followed by support. A statement is followed into the locker room. Are we getting somewhere. A boy inside another boy's mouth is an adjective. Fleshy. Found. A boy inside his own mouth is an argument. A boy on my Netflix account finds his way to another boy's mouth & I am a gestural language I never learned. In the language built for me the past lives behind the body. In the language my body built for me the future lives even if the body does not. The past convinced me that it lives inside the flesh but no one knows its home address. I keep trying to lose it. I keep getting lost in the mail. I keep returning to sender. A boy is an address. A sender is a thesis statement. A boy addresses you. Now we are getting somewhere. Point to where you're heading. Point to where you're coming from. Point to the boy. Now tell me where you live. Are you standing in front of him or behind. Point to which direction you are moving. This logic is circular no one will believe you even if I do.

Sonnet for burial rites
& my firsts night on Grindr

Men send me pictures of their cocks without
moisturizing. & I, left little choice,
must find a way to face the crust of pasts
spread, shed as skin, across their hungry *Nows*.
Their hasty needs. Their powdered power husks,
all musting & all must & all steeped in musk
& inborn androgen & close to blowing
only in the presence of a stiff breeze.
Their dead cell dust: a frumpy cummerbund
around a drunken groom. A dungy bust.
And cumbersome as this small courtesy
may be, trust, we have a history (We)
of taking care to oiling our dead,
that they may disappear into the living.

Background

i learned to speak
i spoke i learned to girl
i learned to speak i learned to girl i learned to still
i learned to speak i learned to girl i learned to lie still
i learned to speak i girled i learned to lie i still i learned to cheat
i spoke girl i learned to lie i learned still still i learned to cheat i learned to spit
i learned to cheat girl i spoke girl i spit spilt i learned to lie i learned to be still i stilled
i learned to lie still sweat i learned to spit i learned to will to wield girl i leaned i learned to cheat
i learned to eat spit split i learned to spit girl i learned to drip sweet i spit i learned to sweat
i learned to sweat i leaned i lied i learned to still i stilled girl i learned to freeze
i still still i leaned to lies still i leaned i learned to spit to sweat freeze
i learned to still girl i lie still girl still i lie beside me
i learned to split i learned to speak
i learned to split spit
i learned to speak

Sonnet for *shaved*
& my chin this time as well

Fuck me raw. I mean. Don't make me wear
my name. I mean. Today I took the blade
to every place my body ends but won't stop
reaching. I mean. I bush & grow. I creep.
I shot my body full of need. I sprout
a man between my hips & on my chin.
He watches me. Rubber bald & blue
screen ready. I steady pitch. I good sharp
scream. My name a wet horizon dream. No
brush weeds. Nothing fuzzing. I cut the blur
from at my edge. I'm even now. I never
even bleed. End myself & lose nothing.
My name. My jaw. My open creasing cleave.
Twin blades I thin to sit inside. Razor clean.

A homily for Abraham
as we prepare the needle

so the story starts   something
about a mountain   a fire

a pyre   an altar   an altered
state   God   or the story   makes

inside the veins
I never read the book   but grew

my limbs inside   a city of fires it set
to show   some lamb   the way

the voice   cracks
before it booms

the story   goes

                to the mirror   to the knife drawer   to the doctor

                to the mouth   around
                the list of side effects

                to the bloodline   with a dull blade
the story goes

to the mountain   Abraham turns him
self around to follow God's

direction lays his only   son
upon the pyre   the monster   moves

28

in the direction   I draw back
    the vile   break   my skin

  & now my sinew as
  the altar   muscle made

  the altar   thickened skin
  the altar   turn myself

    my womb   the altared will
  not choose the pieces of them altered

in this sacrifice   to crack & boom
ing voiced   gods gods

are either fickle or right   or following
direction the monster palms

the tool   the god refused
to grant

I bring
a lamb

& if I am
to make myself

my only
begotten son

then who am I
to sacrifice

To save them both

I learned to run
a chainsaw with seven

men I'd seen feel
the undersides of leaves

behold & whisper
poplar at the light

that shakes silver
then green in the breeze

taught me to watch
the sky throw mare's

tails or lenticular dishes
across itself

& foresee weeping
with all that thunder

& find safety inside
walls we'd asked from trunks

that cradle
our undersides

& whisper
small

the crab apple
outside the office

fell to men
who spent

their days
inside it

engine teeth
& this power

new in their hands
april budding

limbs spread
across the parking lot

another mess
for someone else

to clean up
someone whose time

is worth less
paper

the office
now sharp

against the sky
a grey hollow

as if the tree
once hid the way

the building
refused to flower

as if it bloomed
soft & pink

to save them both

Sonnet for coronation & looks in the locker room

"If a man who thinks he is a king is mad,
a king who thinks he is a king is no less so."
    — Jaques Lacan

Mad King. Finches' kingdom. Birdies built me
crown of sticks with needle tips left over.
Built myself my sovereign even back before this
lip grown velvet. Pin prick magic. Half prick.
Half sweat. Half swagger. Wrong gym bathroom
both ways. Half gone missing. Half left over.
Half the kingdom. King of Halfdom. Halfling King
who'll sing his anthem. Voice, crack against the tile.
Sideways glancing. Never meant to make a scene.
Unsung seen queen. Stuck in your head 'til you
chorus to the manager. Never meant to make a scene.
Me in my royalty. King Halfling of Scenery.
If a man who thinks he is a king is mad,
a king who thinks he is a man--Prove it.

Sonnet for citrus rotting & sexual aversion

I've fucked to find a zipper down men's backs
& some to crawl out sideways from my own.
I drank up all the liquor in your house
& so I lay in bed in waiting now
& eat entire bags of clementines.
I'm turning me to fermentation pit.
I'm DIY. I'm drunk on my own make up.
This time may I forget from inside out.
I turn each wedge in circles on my tongue.
I nearly choke & nearly die alone
& grown & in your bed & what a mess
& while I keep the skin around our flesh,
it holds beneath it sweetness--I am sure
-- & when it splits I know it's nearly gone.

27 explanations for the lump

Once upon a time there was a bear cub
who grew up & out the only way they knew how
& had more teeth than you at the end of it

Once there was a ripe fruit so blood & seed
it could only be named for life or what takes it
& so we called it by grenade or called grenade by it I'm never sure

Once upon a time I bore bare chest at the public pool my mother
bore my ridicule for me see what she lets her daughter
I a wetboy sop with only belly flop sting

Once there was a beechild
never learned to sting just
knew

Once upon a time a ripe fruit grew
lower where a bear reaches ripe fruit falls & life
sometimes sticks to the inside of teeth & gets to rotting

Once a jellyfish grew lumpflesh
& not to hide its stingers but grew stingers as the lumpflesh
sung too soft but needed still its feeding

Once upon a time life made up rotting to take
back pieces it had lost & give & make new
& this is also why it made up teeth

Once a young woman's abdomen grew
outside of her so round the doctors found teeth
inside of it never a voice

Once upon a time you wrote yourself
a name tag in magic marker
you wrote your father's name

Once a blastocyst was the start of you
& all the cells hadn't chosen visions yet or voices could've been
anything could've been not anyway they didn't ask though

Once a bird flew headlong into a window she hadn't
yet learned to believe in what she couldn't see coming
& another & another &

Once in a net a fish names universe
the gills of other soonsoup the sharp
of silver & the sun & the gasping

Once upon a time a bird ate a fish a window
ate the bird a being of ants ate the rotting the clear
sky ate the water from their bodies & the air felt alive

Once infiltrated by contagion a fruit a bird a living
swells outward from a single point fingers tendrils stars
squint it's what the light looks like

Once upon a time you could have been teeth
as much as anything they all start
the same the cells do anyway & storms

Once upon a time your grandmother your aunt your aunt you
had the same feeling feeling something strange in soft & then
fixing a drink wiping a smudge away the wash the windows clean

Once the fermentation starts the jar must be burped
at intervals release the CO_2 shit fizzing of decay
& champagne stings the tongue like kissing dying

Once upon a time your father his sister his sister got the laughs
in the front hall of their mother's wake like grief turns rotting
into bubbles like death likes to make life move for it on its way out

Once a being knows it's dying it will lash out
laugh sing sting decompose pop out pockets of angry
almond shaped fat flesh fibers & keep growing in defiance

Once upon a time your flat chest looked to the world
like the seeds of man the way they say man when they mean human
once you looked like human now look

Once you found the lump you said you'd quit
smoking drinking eating soy gluten much once you stopped
before it stopped the grow before it worked before

Once upon a time a bird flew head long into an airplane
engine hadn't learned yet to believe the wing not
mother

Once they found out the lump was growing they stopped calling
them choices started calling them sensible things to do
when looking at knives

Once upon a time there was a little
there was a child & then woman grew out the side of it
& some parts ripped away

Once the rip comes
open you only wait
until the rotting starts

This is the way life takes
back what has not survived its living
this is the purpose of growth & death & teeth

Once a fruit grows too heavy for a branch it falls

Mimic

I found
my limbs

buried
up

in atmosphere
or serenade

or swallowed
by fingernails

covered in pieces
of livingthing

that kept
growing long

after they
were dead

I dug
up

the boy
fell

the salt
spoke

grave
child

why do you
keep trying

to bow
the ocean

arc
like the sky

don't you
know

that's
the way

a storm
is born

Sonnet for Lifeline & February 2017

& for Kai

It snowed last week & the clouds slept lower.
I wonder where your body went without you.
Who unraveled it & what came falling
from their mouths. I think of you; a weighted
sky; dirt, loosening itself in welcome;
what it is to bury: to deem ready
to give back; to kill: to call a body
just a body, to turn to flesh & name
the rest, the lost, the loft, the fill of us
fever dream prophecies of flightless birds
about the heavens they can't reach. We know
the sky was falling long before these days.
It's just, it seems, the ground thaws out softer
for us now. Hungry or buckling or kind.

Sonnet for heartbreak

the sky the sky the sky the sky the sky
the sky the sky the sky the sky the sky
the sky the sky the sky the sky the sky
the sky the sky the sky the sky the sky
the sky the sky the sky the sky the sky
the sky the sky the sky the sky the sky
the sky the sky the sky the sky the sky
the sky the sky the sky the sky the sky
the swallow the sky the sky the sky the
sky the sky the swallow the sky the sky
the sky the sky the swallow the sky the
sky the sky the sky the sky the swallow
the sky the sky the sky the sky the sky
the sky the sky the sky the sky the sky

After the moonshine
I wake up beside a fern

this morning
in *the heads* of spring
the part that rumor says
will take the sighted's sight
& so we keep for cleaning

I arose inside the barely snowless woods
& climbed my mouth around
an ostrich fern just sprouting from the earth
its furling base a coil tight
with night & need

I close my eyes & opposite of sleep
awaken to the week of warmth
the dew & damp & mostly just the time
it takes (the March)
to coax a wind unbound

that fulls my mouth
to fronds reaching up
& down of me feathered
so my bottom eyelids bursting
with a growing green that climbs to find

the warm the bright
Oh seed Oh sun
Oh supplicant
who prays outstretched & standing
Oh holy song

sung upright & only to the hook
on which the brightest star is hung
there must be some
god that lives
within these lungs

for how you bloom & burst
buried in my throat

Sonnet for respiration & not correcting any of your names for me

A word can suffocate. Same way a Swallow
would, if in the green above the wake
she couldn't trade the wisp of warm she's swollen
with for some cool sliver of this day.
A word is first a certainty that breaks.
A Swallow just a bird & now a bird
a new way & now a breath a new way
& now a surface we can move toward.
Just listen now. A word is first a faith.
Make me beneath your breath & I will change
or rust or burst apart or learn to wait.
They say. They say. They say they say they say
two ways to sink a ship. With gun powder
or with time. Either one you're under water.

In the growing quiet my tinnitus sings to me

Tinnitus: A condition characterized by phantom ringing, hissing, or buzzing in the ears. The pitch of which often corresponds to frequencies in which hearing is impaired, suggesting that the sensation results from overcompensation of the auditory neurons--the brain's reaction to loss: to create sound where sound is perceived as missing.

Translation:

My cherubchild copperhallowed echochamberbasin baby darling
baby hollowstartlestarlingdropindarling baby   i saw you
empty   i found you   out   dripdrained & swallowed
air   froze&open cold &insideyourquiet   you were inside
yourquiet   baby   did you think i'd let you   stay
outthere   inthefreeze   like that   outthere
inthe rubraw air   in the rubberblundersloping hopelessshallow
baby   did you think i'd leave you all   alone   my dear
my darling   holeyhope the sound would slip through   nonono
i came   to fill you   up
fill your empty   spaces   up
to bring   bring   bring the solid stuff together
bring   & bear the barrenboundless out   now   bring i
bring i bring i brought to you this   ringringring   ring
i'm gonna keep the spaces   cemeltedmace
& latelace theraininggrounding   waistinneck & deepdownin now
listen
this binding   ping   this clingtothethreads of the dripdrop
                     listen
clangcling   banging golden echoed seraphim   SERAPHIM spit   squint
spin

swallow fell for a winged throat   hallowedhollow godbloat bring
i brought to you this   ring   this   nailsongtin choirhammers
holyplatedmouthlessvoices openpointed metalpanting   pangsong
dingdin darling   ring   ring   ring ring squint darling squint
not with your eyes with your insides   squint   squint
squint   can you hear   can you hear   can you hear

                              your angels sing
                                      for you i ring

                                              i ring

Sonnet for old ghosts & sound which blankets the earth when finished being heard

You spoke here once & the waves grew wide
& wider still. Until they kissed goodbye
our fingertips & joined the resting *hum,*
the spread left-overs of every *hold me.*
Once. You said *the body is no static*
substance just a momentary place some
come together & each word left bending
air in rippled rings. Away. Away. A
sound will fade. Yes. But I call *nothingness*
a fishing line around a foaming wake.
Call *gone* a body, still, who spits & moves.
The way mine grew to lose the echo sooner.
I mean. We hold what holds us too. I mean.
You disappeared & I still think of you.

On our moon

language will once again be
told to shut up & lick the art forms.
art forms will grow on sink dishes.
dishes will grow inside sinks.
sinks will reproduce sexually
& my small deaf will live next
door to the clanging. hearing will do
dishes in the quiet (carefully). blood will spill
only onto broken plates. we will call out
blood by the name of broken
plates long enough that blood will come
to speak in broken plates.
to the moon-born it will.
to the moon-born, late-deaf
will look like squinted light. broken
dishes will kaleidoscope.
silent will lick the art forms' undersides
& rename itself space,
will fill lunch bags
up with broken dishes,
bring them out to parties.
parties will be other names for deaths
births & nap-taking.
Nap-taking will ask for fingertips
at the door & bury them
in velvet cords & the asking
will be done in a light language.
shattered glass, crystal, or needing to know.

My cock & my tits invite 16-year-old me to tea in effort to offer advice on the future & don't bring sandwiches because they know I won't eat them

it all changes

     tell him

not all of it

     we haven't figured out how much

yet

     yet

won't

     that changes

you become a marble statue

     one with the nice tits

nice tits & then grow life

     you're not flesh so much as stone living

you're carved perfect & ruin it dancing

you sprout peacock ferns in your palms

        & love with their browning

you cry & moss grows

        someone draws you

in the afternoon

        & thinks they bring you home

you cry to see yourself remembered

        don't like they way it holds still

you cry & moss grows

        know your arms by the fished rivers you've carved in them

your now scabbing grows your stone to once flesh

        these are your children

see kid it's complicated

        complicated

it all changes

        the parts you think will stay

& none you think will not

        oh have some tea darling

forgive me for going on

        oh go on you must be petrified

dear you must

      you must darling

            you must

Sonnet for *Streptococcus pyogenes* & second puberty

I pray for the microbes inside of me.
Fit my mouth around a garden full of
family trees. Children's children. 12 hours to
live/split/live again. I, for the third time
this summer, swallow their tombs with coffee
& warm Modelo. I'm not supposed to
drink, but every coming of age needs a
little rebellion. Vocal chords, open
as an eighth-grade sundown with nowhere
good to be. Voice, new-deep enough to leave
room for bad influence. But what can grow
without a million tears apart. Each small
enough to live inside. I pray for what
comes home in me. For what lives. For what dies.

Notes

"Meaning" is comprised almost entirely of first page Google results for the search "definition swallow"

"Sonnet for cock sucking & baptism" is informed by lessons I learned about the body from Janani Balasubramanian's essay *"How Many Licks"*

The epigraph to "Sonnet for my coronation & looks in the locker room" is a quote I originally encountered in Maggie Smith's *The Argonauts*

"A homily for Abraham as we prepare the needle" was written in a workshop led by Safia Elhillo for Winter Tangerine

"In the growing quiet my tinnitus sings to me" was written in a workshop led by Justice Ameer

"TV is making movies about gay teenagers..." is after Richard Siken

"The Spandrels of San Marco OR If I should come to say the empty call my own name back at me instead" explores concepts from the essay "The spandrels of San Marco and the Panglossian paradigm: a critique of the adaptationist programme" by Stephen Jay Gould and Richard C. Lewontin

Acknowledgments

Sincere thanks to the editors of publications in which versions of some of these poems have appeared or are forthcoming:

"Sonnet for speech too soft & you who've yet to choose a name" in *Glass: A Journal of Poetry;*

"Sonnet for cock sucking & baptism" and "Sonnet for sonic feedback & media representation" in *Muzzle;*

"Sonnet for eating & hormone injection" and "Sonnet for *Streptococcus pyogenes* and second puberty" in *The Journal;*

"Sonnet for Trans Lifeline and February 2017" in *Voicemail Poems;*

"In the growing quiet my Tinnitus sings to me" in *Sonora Review;*

"*The Spandrels at San Marco*" in *Deaf Poets Society;*

"To save them both" in *The Thalweg;*

"27 explanations for the lump" in *The Shallow Ends;*

"On our moon" in *Drunk in a Midnight Choir.*

Thank you Golden, for texting to remind me of the open reading period deadline. I'm so grateful for you, my friend, your brilliance, your generosity, and your keen awareness of calendars.

Thank you to Sibling Rivalry Press, Seth Pennington, and Aidan Forster, and especially to Bryan Borland. I could not have asked for a better team and I am so grateful to be part of yours.

To Jess Rizkallah and torrin a. greathouse, for your thoughtful and careful edits that turned this work from parts into a whole.

To the friends and artists and spaces who have shaped these poems and the life I live around them: My Kings, Jeff, Matt, Jed, Bre, Lou, and Mamba, who make our home a home and a home so filled with possibilities. It is all my dreams come true. To my water brothers, Wilkie and Heuser, for making sure I am the opposite of lost. To Olivia Gatwood for many games of "this word or that word," for treating my work with so much care and for open source therapeutic intervention for struggling fish. To Porsha Olayiwola for work dates and reminding me this is all magic. To the artists and writers who make up the substance of my mind and my life. I am so lucky to know all of my heroes: Emil Eastman, Raven McGill, Melissa Lozada-Oliva, Daniel Cohen, Anthony Christiano, Zenaida Peterson, Oompa, Marshall Gillson, Anjimile, Janae Johnson, Ashley Davis, Christopher Clauss, Chrysanthemum Tran, Ewan Hill, John-Francis Quiñonez, Justice Ameer, Muggs Fogarty, Robbie Dunning, Charlotte Abotsi, Illyus Evander, Jonathan Mendoza, Emmanuel Oppong-Yeboah, Rebecca Lynn, Red, Tatiana Johnson-Boria, Erich Haygun, JR Mahung, Claudia Wilson, Sam Chin, Alex Charalambides, George Abraham, Bradley Trumpfeller, Sara Mae Henke, Brandon Melendez, James Miranda, Julissa Emile, Cassandra de Alba, Catherine Weiss, Simone Beaubien, Mark Palos, Mckendy Fils-Aimé, Will James, Emily Myers, Tyler Torolla, Claire Siesfeld, David & Mike Runge, Nikk & Christine Foltz, Kathleen Maris Paltrineri, Ben Ben Ami, Shadi Habib Allah. To Hanif Abdurraqib, Safia Elhillo, Hieu Mihn Nguyen, Meg Day, Franny Choi, Ilya Kaminsky, Danez Smith, Sam Sax, Cameron Awkward Rich, for your work and your encouragement, which meant so much to me. To Newcomb Greenleaf, Sui Yee Wong, Bobby Buchanan, Walter Butts, Michael Vizsolyi, Goddard College, Slam Free or Die, The House Slam, The Boston Poetry Slam, FEMS, The Haley House Bakery & Café,

MASSLeap, Make Shift Boston, Poets House, *Winter Tangerine*, The Gabrielle Bouliane Foundation, The YMCA, and to The Nashua Public Library, which has ordered almost all of the weird, gay poetry I have requested.

To my teachers, Christine Stearns, Brett Salamin, Sue Messenger, Marie Becker, Charles Balkcom, and Elena Moran for somehow keeping me alive through adolescence.

To the Rhoades family for growing with me and around me.

To my family, my mom, Astrid, who always knew I was a poet, and to Pops, Alana, and Sean, for the whole world each of you has taught me. I couldn't be luckier.

I am so grateful for all of you. And you, I am so grateful for you. I am grateful. I am so grateful.

The Poet

Sam Rush began writing poems after developing progressive hearing loss and realizing how many words each word could be.

The Press

Sibling Rivalry Press is an independent press based in Little Rock, Arkansas. It is a sponsored project of Fractured Atlas, a nonprofit arts service organization. Contributions to support the operations of Sibling Rivalry Press are tax-deductible to the extent permitted by law, and your donations will directly assist in the publication of work that disturbs and enraptures. To contribute to the publication of more books like this one, please visit our website and click *donate*.

Printed in the USA
CPSIA information can be obtained
at www.ICGtesting.com
LVHW091621120424
777081LV00006B/441